U.S. Department
of Transportation

**Federal Aviation
Administration**

FAA-S-8081-9D
with Changes 1 & 2

FLIGHT INSTRUCTOR

INSTRUMENT

Practical Test Standards

for

AIRPLANE

and

HELICOPTER

July 2010

FLIGHT STANDARDS SERVICE
Washington, DC 20591

FLIGHT INSTRUCTOR INSTRUMENT

Practical Test Standards

for

AIRPLANE

and

HELICOPTER

2010

FLIGHT STANDARDS SERVICE
Washington, DC 20591

NOTE

Material in FAA-S-8081-9D will be effective July 1, 2010. All previous editions of the Flight Instructor—Instrument Practical Test Standards will be obsolete as of this date.

MAJOR ENHANCEMENTS

Introduction:

1. Added abbreviations
2. Special Emphasis Areas—updated
3. Replaced APV note with LPV verbiage in Aircraft and Equipment Required for the Practical Test section
4. Deleted Aeronautical Decision Making and Risk Management and replaced with Single-Pilot Resource Management
5. Emphasis on Attitude Instrument Flying and Partial Panel Skills—updated
6. Renewal or Reinstatement of a Flight Instructor—Task L changed to Task D
7. Added section titled Use of the Judgment Assessment Matrix

Examiner's Practical Test Checklist

Item I. H. deleted.

Area of Operations

1. AREA OF OPERATION I, Task B, Objective updated
2. AREA OF OPERATION I, Task D, added item 7 to include scenario based training method
3. AREA OF OPERATION IX, Task D, added Multiengine to the Task title

Appendices

1. Appendix 1 introduction—updated
2. Added Appendices 2 and 3

RECORD OF CHANGES

Change 1 – 5/3/2012

- Appendix 1, deleted columns 1, 2, and 3
- Deleted Appendix 2: Non-FSTD Credit

Change 2 – 4/18/2014

- Added "Instructor" to the title of the *Addition of an Instrument Rating to a Flight Instructor Certificate* table (page 20)
- Removed the Glider ("G") column from the *Addition of an Instrument Instructor Rating to a Flight Instructor Certificate* table and revised the Legend (page 20)

FOREWORD

The Flight Instructor—Instrument Practical Test Standards (PTS) book has been published by the Federal Aviation Administration (FAA) to establish the standards for flight instructor certification and instrument rating practical tests for airplanes and helicopters. FAA inspectors and designated pilot examiners shall conduct practical tests in compliance with these standards. Flight instructors and applicants should find these standards helpful during training and when preparing for the practical test.

/s/ 5-03-2010

_____
Van Kerns, Manager
Regulatory Support Division
Flight Standards Service

FAA-S-8081-9D

CONTENTS

INTRODUCTION 1

    General Information 1
    Practical Test Standard Concept 2
    Flight Instructor Practical Test Book Description 2
    Abbreviations 5
    Use of the Practical Test Standards 6
    Use of the Judgment Assessment Matrix 7
    Special Emphasis Areas 8
    Aircraft and Equipment Required for the Practical Test 8
    Use of FAA-Approved Flight Simulation Training Device (FSTD) . 10
    Flight Instructor Responsibility 11
    Examiner Responsibility 12
    Satisfactory Performance 13
    Unsatisfactory Performance 13
    Letter of Discontinuance 14
    Single-Pilot Resource Management 14
        1. Aeronautical Decision Making 15
        2. Risk Management 15
        3. Task Management 16
        4. Situational Awareness 16
        5. Controlled Flight Into Terrain Awareness 17
        6. Automation Management 17
    Applicant's Use of Checklists 18
    Use of Distractions During Practical Tests 18
    Positive Exchange of Flight Controls 18
    Emphasis on Attitude Instrument Flying and Partial Panel
    Skills 19
    Addition of an Instrument Rating to a Flight Instructor
    Certificate 20
    Renewal or Reinstatement of a Flight Instructor 21

CHECKLISTS

    Applicant's Practical Test Checklist 1-i
    Examiner's Practical Test Checklist 1-iii

AREAS OF OPERATION

I. FUNDAMENTALS OF INSTRUCTING

    A. Learning Process 1-1
    B. Human Behavior and Effective Communication 1-1
    C. Teaching Process 1-2
    D. Teaching Methods 1-2
    E. Critique and Evaluation 1-2
    F. Flight Instructor Characteristics and Responsibilities 1-3
    G. Planning Instructional Activity 1-3

II. TECHNICAL SUBJECT AREAS

    A. Aircraft Flight Instruments and Navigation Equipment 1-4
    B. Aeromedical Factors 1-5
    C. Regulations and Publications Related to IFR Operations ... 1-5
    D. Logbook Entries Related to Instrument Instruction 1-6

III. PREFLIGHT PREPARATION

    A. Weather Information 1-7
    B. Cross-Country Flight Planning 1-8
    C. Instrument Cockpit Check 1-8

IV. PREFLIGHT LESSON ON A MANEUVER TO BE PERFORMED IN FLIGHT

    A. Maneuver Lesson 1-10

V. AIR TRAFFIC CONTROL CLEARANCES AND PROCEDURES

    A. Air Traffic Control Clearances 1-11
    B. Compliance With Departure, En Route, and Arrival Procedures and Clearances 1-11

VI. FLIGHT BY REFERENCE TO INSTRUMENTS

    A. Straight-and-Level Flight 1-12
    B. Turns 1-13
    C. Change of Airspeed in Straight-and-Level and Turning Flight 1-14
    D. Constant Airspeed Climbs and Descents 1-15
    E. Constant Rate Climbs and Descents 1-16
    F. Timed Turns to Magnetic Compass Headings 1-17
    G. Steep Turns 1-18
    H. Recovery From Unusual Flight Attitudes 1-19

VII. NAVIGATION SYSTEMS

    A. Intercepting and Tracking Navigational Systems and DME Arcs 1-20
    B. Holding Procedures 1-21

VIII. INSTRUMENT APPROACH PROCEDURES

    A. Nonprecision Instrument Approach 1-22
    B. Precision Instrument Approach 1-24
    C. Missed Approach 1-25
    D. Circling Approach (Airplane) 1-26
    E. Landing From a Straight-In Approach 1-27

IX. EMERGENCY OPERATIONS

 A Loss of Communications 1-28
 B. Approach With Loss of Primary Flight Instrument Indicators 1-28
 C. Engine Failure During Straight-and-Level Flight and Turns 1-29
 D. Instrument Approach—One Engine Inoperative 1-30

X. POSTFLIGHT PROCEDURES

 A. Checking Instruments and Equipment 1-32

APPENDIX 1: FLIGHT SIMULATION TRAINING DEVICE CREDIT

Task vs. Flight Simulation Training Device (FSTD) Credit A1-1
Use of Chart A1-1
Flight Simulation Training Device (FSTD) Level A1-2

APPENDIX 2: NON-FSTD CREDIT

Task vs. Non-FSTD Credit (Other Training Devices) A2-1
Use of Chart A2-1
Non-FSTD Level A2-2

APPENDIX 3: JUDGMENT ASSESSMENT MATRIX: FLIGHT INSTRUCTOR INSTRUMENT

Judgment Assessment Matrix A3-1
Purpose of the Assessment A3-2
Directions for Completion of the Assessment A3-2
Definitions of Resource Management Areas A3-2

INTRODUCTION

General Information

The Flight Standards Service of the Federal Aviation Administration (FAA) has developed this practical test book as the standard that must be used by FAA examiners[1] when conducting flight instructor—instrument (airplane and helicopter) practical tests. Flight instructors are expected to use this book when preparing applicants for practical tests. Applicants should be familiar with this book and become familiar with these standards during their training.

It is important to note that pilot training must not be limited solely to meeting the TASKS and Objectives in this book. TASKS and Objectives are simply means to determine if an applicant meets the regulatory standards for the certificate or rating sought. Applicants should be trained using the references cited in this book.

The FAA gratefully acknowledges the valuable assistance provided by many industry participants who contributed their time and talent in assisting with the revision of these practical test standards.

This practical test standard (PTS) may be purchased from the Superintendent of Documents, U.S. Government Printing Office (GPO), Washington, DC 20402-9325, or from http://bookstore.gpo.gov. This PTS is also available for download, in pdf format, from the Flight Standards Service web site at www.faa.gov.

This PTS is published by the U.S. Department of Transportation, Federal Aviation Administration, Airman Testing Standards Branch, AFS-630, P.O. Box 25082, Oklahoma City, OK 73125. Comments regarding this book should be sent in e-mail form to AFS630comments@faa.gov.

---

[1] The word "examiner" denotes either the FAA inspector, FAA designated pilot examiner, or other authorized person who conducts the practical test.

Practical Test Standard Concept

Title 14 of the Code of Federal Regulations (14 CFR) part 61 specifies the areas in which knowledge and skill must be demonstrated by the applicant before the issuance of a flight instructor certificate with the associated category and class ratings. The CFRs provide the flexibility to permit the FAA to publish practical test standards containing the AREAS OF OPERATION and specific TASKS in which competency shall be demonstrated. The FAA will revise this book whenever it is determined that changes are needed in the interest of safety. *Adherence to the provisions of the regulations and the practical test standards is mandatory for the evaluation of flight instructor applicants.*

Flight Instructor Practical Test Book Description

This test book contains the practical test standards for flight instructor—instrument (airplane and helicopter).

The flight instructor practical test standards include the AREAS OF OPERATION and TASKS required for the issuance of an initial flight instructor certificate and for the addition of a category and/or class rating to that certificate.

AREAS OF OPERATION are phases of the practical test arranged in a logical sequence within each standard. They begin with Fundamentals of Instructing and end with Postflight Procedures. The examiner, however, may conduct the practical test in any sequence that will result in a complete and efficient test; however, *the ground portion of the practical test must be completed prior to the flight portion.*

TASKS are titles of knowledge areas, flight procedures, or maneuvers appropriate to an AREA OF OPERATION.

NOTE is used to emphasize special considerations required in the AREA OF OPERATION or TASK.

REFERENCE(S) identifies the publication(s) that describe(s) the TASK. Descriptions of TASKS and maneuver tolerances are not included in these standards because this information can be found in the current issue of the listed references. Publications other than those listed may be used for references if their content conveys substantially the same meaning as the referenced publications.

These practical test standards are based on the following references:

14 CFR Part 1	Definitions and Abbreviations
14 CFR Part 23	Airworthiness Standards: Normal, Utility, Acrobatic, and Commuter Category Airplanes
14 CFR Part 39	Airworthiness Directives
14 CFR Part 43	Maintenance, Preventive Maintenance, Rebuilding, and Alteration
14 CFR Part 61	Certification: Pilots, Flight Instructors, and Ground Instructors
14 CFR Part 67	Medical Standards and Certification
14 CFR Part 71	Designation of Class A, B, C, D, and E Airspace Areas; Air Traffic Service Routes, and Reporting Points
14 CFR Part 91	General Operating and Flight Rules
14 CFR Part 95	IFR Altitudes
14 CFR Part 97	Standard Instrument Procedures
NTSB Part 830	Notification and Reporting of Aircraft Accidents and Incidents
AC 00-2	Advisory Circular Checklist
AC 00-6	Aviation Weather for Pilots and Flight Operations Personnel
AC 00-45	Aviation Weather Services
AC 60-22	Aeronautical Decision Making
AC 60-28	English Language Skill Standards Required by 14 CFR Parts 61, 63, and 65
AC 61-65	Certification: Pilots and Flight Instructors
AC 61-84	Role of Preflight Preparation
AC 61-98	Currency and Additional Qualification Requirements for Certificated Pilots
AC 90-42	Traffic Advisory Practices at Airports Without Operating Control Towers
AC 90-48	Pilots' Role in Collision Avoidance
AC 90-66	Recommended Standard Traffic Patterns for Aeronautical Operations at Airports Without Operating Control Towers
AC 90-105	Approval of Guidance for RNP Operations and Barometric Vertical Navigation in the U.S. National Airspace System
AC 120-51	Crew Resource Management Training
FAA-H-8083-1	Weight and Balance Handbook
FAA-H-8083-9	Aviation Instructor's Handbook
FAA-H-8083-15	Instrument Flying Handbook
FAA-H-8083-25	Pilot's Handbook of Aeronautical Knowledge
FAA-S-8081-4	Instrument Rating Practical Test Standards
FAA Order 8080.6	Conduct of Airman Knowledge Tests
AIM	Aeronautical Information Manual
AFD	Airport/Facility Directory

IAPs	Instrument Approach Procedures
DPs	Departure Procedures
STARs	Standard Terminal Arrivals
NOTAMs	Notices to Airmen
Others	Enroute Low Altitude Charts
	Appropriate aircraft flight manuals
	FAA-approved flight manual supplements

The Objective lists the important elements that must be satisfactorily performed to demonstrate competency in a TASK. The Objective includes:

1. Specifically what the applicant should be able to do,
2. Conditions under which the TASK is to be performed, and
3. Acceptable performance standards.

The examiner determines that the applicant meets the TASK Objective through the demonstration of competency in various elements of knowledge and/or skill. The Objectives of TASKS in certain AREAS OF OPERATION, such as Fundamentals of Instructing and Technical Subjects, include only knowledge elements. Objectives of TASKS in AREAS OF OPERATION that include elements of skill, as well as knowledge, also include common errors, which the applicant shall be able to describe, recognize, analyze, and correct.

The Objective of a TASK that involves pilot skill consists of four parts. The four parts include determination that the applicant exhibits:

1. Instructional knowledge of the elements of a TASK. This is accomplished through descriptions, explanations, and simulated instruction;
2. Instructional knowledge of common errors related to a TASK, including their recognition, analysis, and correction;
3. The ability to demonstrate and simultaneously explain the key elements of a TASK. The TASK demonstration must be to the INSTRUMENT PILOT skill level; the teaching techniques and procedures should conform to those set forth in FAA-H-8083-9, Aviation Instructor's Handbook, and FAA-H-8083-15, Instrument Flying Handbook; and
4. The ability to analyze and correct common errors related to a TASK.

Abbreviations

14 CFR	Title 14 of the Code of Federal Regulations
ADF	Automatic Direction Finder
ADM	Aeronautical Decision Making
AFD	Airport/Facility Directory
AIRMET	Airman's Meteorological Information
AM	Automation Management
APV	Approach With Vertical Guidance
ATC	Air Traffic Control
ATIS	Automatic Terminal Information
ATS	Air Traffic Service
CDI	Course Deviation Indicator
CFIT	Controlled Flight Into Terrain
CRM	Crew Resource Management
DA/DH	Decision Altitude/Decision Height
DH	Decision Height
DME	Distance Measuring Equipment
DP	Departure Procedures
EGPWS	Enhanced Ground Proximity Warning System
FAA	Federal Aviation Administration
FDC	Flight Data Center
FITS	FAA-Industry Training Standards
FMS	Flight Management System
FSDO	Flight Standards District Office
GLS	GNSS Landing System
GNSS	Global Navigation Satellite System
GPO	Government Printing Office
GPS	Global Positioning System
GPWS	Ground Proximity Warning System
IAP	Instrument Approach Procedures
IFR	Instrument Flight Rules
ILS	Instrument Landing System
IMC	Instrument Meteorological Conditions
LAHSO	Land and Hold Short Operations
LCD	Liquid Crystal Display
LDA	Localizer-Type Directional Aid
LED	Light-Emitting Diode
LNAV	Lateral Navigation
LOC	Localizer
LORAN	Long Range Navigation
LPV	Localizer Performance With Vertical Guidance
MAP	Missed Approach Point
MDA	Minimum Descent Altitude
MLS	Microwave Landing System
NAS	National Airspace System
NAVAID	Navigation Aid
NDB	Nondirectional Beacon
NOTAM	Notice to Airmen
NPA	Nonprecision Approach
NWS	National Weather Service
OCS	Obstacle Clearance Surface

OEA	Obstacle Evaluation Area
PA	Precision Approach
PC	Proficiency Check
PTS	Practical Test Standard
RAIM	Receiver Autonomous Integrity Monitoring
RM	Risk Management
RMI	Radio Magnetic Indicator
RNAV	Area Navigation
RNP	Required Navigation Performance
SA	Situational Awareness
SAAAR	Special Aircraft and Aircrew Authorization Required
SAS	Stability Augmentation System
SDF	Simplified Directional Facility
SIGMETS	Significant Meteorological Advisory
SRM	Single Pilot Resource Management
STAR	Standard Terminal Arrival
TAWS	Terrain Awareness and Warning System
TCAS	Traffic Alert and Collision Avoidance System
TM	Task Management
VDP	Visual Descent Point
VHF	Very High Frequency
VNAV	Vertical Navigation
VOR	Very High Frequency Omnidirectional Range

Use of the Practical Test Standards

The FAA requires that all flight instructor practical tests be conducted in accordance with the appropriate flight instructor practical test standards and the policies set forth in the INTRODUCTION.

All of the procedures and maneuvers in the instrument rating practical test standards have been included in the flight instructor practical test standards; however, to permit completion of the practical test for initial certification within a reasonable time-frame, the examiner shall select one or more TASKS in each AREA OF OPERATION. In certain AREAS OF OPERATION, there are required TASKS that the examiner must select. These required TASKS are identified by a **NOTE** immediately following each AREA OF OPERATION title.

In preparation for each practical test, the examiner shall prepare a written "plan of action." The plan of action includes a scenario. The examiner must develop a scenario that allows the evaluation of most of the AREAS OF OPERATIONS and TASKS required in the practical tests with minimum disruptions. During the mission, the examiner interjects problems and emergencies that the applicant must handle. It should be structured so that most of the AREAS OF OPERATIONS and TASKS are accomplished within the mission. The examiner must maintain the flexibility to change the plan due to unexpected situations as they arise and still result in an efficient and valid test. Some tasks (e.g., unusual attitudes) are not normally done during routine flight operations or may not fit into the scenario. These maneuvers still must be demonstrated. It is preferable that these maneuvers be demonstrated after the scenario is completed. But, the practical test scenario can be suspended to do maneuvers, and resumed if the situation, due to time and efficiency of the practical test, dictates so. ***Any TASK selected for evaluation during a practical test shall be evaluated in its entirety.***

Applicant shall be expected to perform TASK H in AREA OF OPERATION VI, Recovery from Unusual Attitudes and TASK A in AREA OF OPERATION VIII, Nonprecision Instrument Approach using a view-limiting device.

The flight instructor applicant shall be prepared in *all* knowledge and skill areas and demonstrate the ability to instruct effectively in *all* TASKS included in the AREAS OF OPERATION of this practical test standard. Throughout the flight portion of the practical test, the examiner shall evaluate the applicant's ability to demonstrate and simultaneously explain the selected procedures and maneuvers, and to give flight instruction to students at various stages of flight training and levels of experience.

The term "instructional knowledge" means that the flight instructor applicant's discussions, explanations, and descriptions should follow the recommended teaching procedures and techniques explained in FAA-H-8083-9, Aviation Instructor's Handbook. This includes the development of scenario-based lessons, the ability to evaluate single pilot resource management (SRM) skills, and the ability to use learner-centered grading.

The purpose of including common errors in certain TASKS is to assist the examiner in determining that the flight instructor applicant has the ability to recognize, analyze, and correct such errors. The examiner will not simulate any condition that may jeopardize safe flight or result in possible damage to the aircraft. The common errors listed in the TASKS objective may or may not be found in the TASK References. However, the FAA considers their frequency of occurrence justification for inclusion in the TASK Objectives.

Use of the Judgment Assessment Matrix

Most fatal accident include a lack of SRM skills (task management (TM), risk management (RM), automation management (AM), aeronautical decision making (ADM), controlled flight into terrain (CFIT), and situational awareness (SA)) as a causal factor. Consequently, examiners must evaluate the applicant to ensure that he or she has the appropriate level of these skills. A Judgment Assessment Matrix is provided as a tool to evaluate the applicant's SRM skills objectively. The examiner will use the Judgment Assessment Matrix during the practical test. Since examiners give multiple tests, it is recommended that examiners make photocopies of the matrix.

Special Emphasis Areas

Examiners shall place special emphasis upon areas of aircraft operations considered critical to flight safety. Among these are:

1. Positive aircraft control;
2. Positive exchange of the flight controls procedure (who is flying the aircraft);
3. Stall/spin awareness;
4. Collision avoidance;
5. Wake turbulence avoidance;
6. Land and Hold Short Operations (LAHSO);
7. Runway incursion avoidance;
8. CFIT;
9. ADM and RM;
10. Checklist usage;
11. SRM;
12. Icing condition operational hazards, anti-icing and deicing equipment, differences, and approved use and operations;
13. required navigation performance (RNP);
14. crew resource management (CRM) for multi-pilot aircraft; and
15. Other areas deemed appropriate to any phase of the practical test.

With the exception of SRM, any given area may not be addressed specifically under a TASK, but all areas are essential to flight safety and will be evaluated during the practical test.

Aircraft and Equipment Required for the Practical Test

The flight instructor—instrument applicant is required by 14 CFR part 61 to provide an airworthy, certificated aircraft for use during the practical test. Its operating limitations must not prohibit the TASKS required on the practical test. This section further requires that the aircraft must:

1. Have fully functioning dual controls, and;
2. Be capable of performing all AREAS OF OPERATION appropriate for the instructor rating sought and have no operating limitations, which prohibit its use in any of the AREAS OF OPERATION, required for the practical test.

Flight instruments are those required for controlling the aircraft without outside references. The required radio equipment is that which is necessary for communications with air traffic control (ATC), and for the performance of two of the following nonprecision approaches: very high frequency omnidirectional range (VOR), nondirectional beacon (NDB), global positioning system (GPS) without vertical guidance, localizer (LOC), localizer-type directional aid (LDA), simplified directional facility (SDF), or area navigation (RNAV) and one precision approach: instrument landing system (ILS), GNSS landing system (GLS), localizer performance with vertical guidance (LPV) or microwave landing system (MLS). GPS equipment must be instrument certified and contain the current database. Note: An LPV approach is technically a nonprecision approach, however, due to the precision of its glidepath and localizer-like lateral navigation characteristics, an LPV can be used to demonstrate precision approach proficiency (AOA VIII TASK B). Also, although LPV and LNAV/VNAV approaches are nonprecision approaches, they cannot be used to demonstrate nonprecision approach proficiency (AOA VIII TASK A) due to the presence of a glidepath.

Modern technology has introduced into aviation a new method of displaying flight instruments, such as Electronic Flight Instrument Systems, Integrated Flight Deck displays, and others. For the purpose of the practical test standards, any flight instrument display that utilizes liquid crystal display (LCD) or picture-tube-like displays will be referred to as "Electronic Flight Instrument Display." Aircraft equipped with this technology may or may not have separate backup flight instruments installed. The abnormal or emergency procedure for loss of the electronic flight instrument display appropriate to the aircraft will be evaluated in the Loss of Primary Instruments TASK. The loss of the primary electronic flight instrument display must be tailored to failures that would normally be encountered in the aircraft. If the aircraft is capable, total failure of the electronic flight instrument display, or a supporting component, with access only to the standby flight instruments or backup display shall be evaluated.

The applicant is required to provide an appropriate view limiting device that is acceptable to the examiner. This device shall be used during all testing that requires testing "solely by reference to instruments." This device must prevent the applicant from having visual reference outside the aircraft, but not prevent the examiner from having visual reference outside the aircraft. A procedure should be established between the applicant and the examiner as to when and how this device should be donned and removed and this procedure should be briefed before the flight.

The applicant is expected to utilize an autopilot and/or flight management system (FMS), if properly installed, during the flight instructor—instrument practical test to assist in the management of the aircraft. The examiner is expected to test the applicant's knowledge of the systems that are installed and operative during the oral and flight portions of the practical test. The applicant will be required to demonstrate the use of the autopilot and/or FMS during one of the nonprecision approaches. The applicant is expected to demonstrate satisfactory automation management skills.

If the practical test is conducted in the aircraft, and the aircraft has an operable and properly installed GPS, the examiner will require and the applicant must demonstrate GPS approach proficiency. If the applicant has contracted for training in an approved course that includes GPS training in the system that is installed in the airplane/simulator/FTD and the airplane/simulator/FTD used for the checking/testing has the same system properly installed and operable, the applicant must demonstrate GPS approach proficiency.

NOTE: For GPS, add RNP when applicable.

NOTE: If any avionics/navigation unit, including GPS, in the aircraft used for the practical test is placarded inoperative, the examiner will review the maintenance log to verify that the discrepancy has been properly documented.

Use of FAA-Approved Flight Simulation Training Device (FSTD)

An airman applicant for instrument rating certification is authorized to use a full flight simulator (FFS) qualified by the National Simulator Program as levels A–D and/or a flight training device (FTD) qualified by the National Simulator Program as levels 4–7 to complete certain flight TASK requirements listed in this practical test standard.

In order to do so, such devices must be used pursuant to and in accordance with a curriculum approved for use at a 14 CFR part 141 pilot school or 14 CFR part 142 training center. Practical tests or portions thereof, when accomplished in an FSTD, may only be conducted by FAA aviation safety inspectors, designees authorized to conduct such tests in FSTDs for part 141 pilot school graduates, or appropriately authorized part 142 Training Center Evaluators (TCE).

When flight TASKS are accomplished in an aircraft, certain TASK elements may be accomplished through "simulated" actions in the interest of safety and practicality, but when accomplished in a flight simulator or flight training device, these same actions would not be "simulated." For example, when in an aircraft, a simulated engine fire may be addressed by retarding the throttle to idle, simulating the shutdown of the engine, simulating the discharge of the fire suppression agent, if applicable, simulating the disconnection of associated electrical, hydraulic, and pneumatics systems. However, when the same emergency condition is addressed in a FSTD, all TASK elements must be accomplished as would be expected under actual circumstances.

Similarly, safety of flight precautions taken in the aircraft for the accomplishment of a specific maneuver or procedure (such as limiting altitude in an approach to stall or setting maximum airspeed for an engine failure expected to result in a rejected takeoff) need not be taken when a FSTD is used.

It is important to understand that, whether accomplished in an aircraft or FSTD, all TASKS and elements for each maneuver or procedure shall have the same performance standards applied equally for determination of overall satisfactory performance.

The applicant must demonstrate all of the instrument approach procedures required by 14 CFR part 61. At least one instrument approach procedure must be demonstrated in an airplane, helicopter, or powered lift as appropriate. One precision and one nonprecision approach not selected for actual flight demonstration may be performed in FSTDs that meet the requirements of Appendix 1 of this practical test standard.

Flight Instructor Responsibility

An appropriately rated flight instructor is responsible for training the flight instructor applicant to acceptable standards in *all* subject matter areas, procedures, and maneuvers included in the TASKS within each AREA OF OPERATION in the appropriate flight instructor practical test standard.

Because of the impact of their teaching activities in developing safe, proficient pilots, flight instructors should exhibit a high level of knowledge, skill, and the ability to impart that knowledge and skill to students. The flight instructor shall certify that the applicant is:

1. Able to make a practical application of the fundamentals of instructing;
2. Competent to teach the subject matter, procedures, and maneuvers included in the standards to students with varying backgrounds and levels of experience and ability;
3. Able to perform the procedures and maneuvers included in the standards to the INSTRUMENT PILOT skill level while giving effective flight instruction; and
4. Competent to pass the required practical test for the issuance of the flight instructor certificate with the associated category and class ratings or the addition of a category and/or class rating to a flight instructor certificate.

Throughout the applicant's training, the flight instructor is responsible for emphasizing the performance of, and the ability to teach, *effective visual scanning, runway incursion avoidance, collision avoidance procedures, and LAHSO.* The flight instructor applicant should develop and use scenario based teaching methods particularly on special emphasis areas. These areas are covered in AC 90-48, Pilot's Role in Collision Avoidance; FAA-H-8083-3, Airplane Flying Handbook; FAA-H-8083-25, Pilot's Handbook of Aeronautical Knowledge; and the current Aeronautical Information Manual.

Examiner Responsibility

The examiner conducting the practical test is responsible for determining that the applicant meets acceptable standards of teaching ability, knowledge, and skill in the selected TASKS. The examiner makes this determination by accomplishing an Objective that is appropriate to each selected TASK, and includes an evaluation of the applicant's:

1. Ability to apply the fundamentals of instructing;
2. Knowledge of, and ability to teach, the subject matter, procedures, and maneuvers covered in the TASKS;
3. Ability to perform the procedures and maneuvers included in the standards to the INSTRUMENT PILOT skill level while giving effective flight instruction;
4. Ability to analyze and correct common errors related to the procedures and maneuvers covered in the TASKS;
5. Ability to develop scenario-based instruction that meets lesson objectives;
6. Ability to teach and evaluate SRM and CRM, to include multi-pilot aircraft; and
7. Ability to use learner-centered grading and debriefing techniques appropriately.

It is intended that oral questioning be used at any time during the ground or flight portion of the practical test to determine that the applicant can instruct effectively and has a comprehensive knowledge of the TASKS and their related safety factors.

During the flight portion of the practical test, the examiner shall act as a student during selected maneuvers. This will give the examiner an opportunity to evaluate the flight instructor applicant's ability to analyze and correct simulated common errors related to these maneuvers. The examiner will also evaluate the applicant's use of visual scanning and collision avoidance procedures, and the applicant's ability to teach those procedures.

Examiners should, to the greatest extent possible, test the applicant's application and correlation skills. When possible, scenario based questions should be used.

The examiner shall place special emphasis on the applicant's demonstrated ability to teach precise aircraft control and sound judgment in aeronautical decision making. Evaluation of the applicant's ability to teach judgment shall be accomplished by asking the applicant to describe the oral discussions and the presentation of practical problems that would be used in instructing students in the exercise of sound judgment. The examiner shall also emphasize the evaluation of the applicant's demonstrated ability to teach spatial disorientation, wake turbulence and low-level wind shear avoidance, checklist usage, positive exchange of flight controls, and any other directed special emphasis areas.

FAA-S-8081-9D

Satisfactory Performance

The practical test is passed if, in the judgment of the examiner, the applicant demonstrates satisfactory performance with regard to:

1. Knowledge of the fundamentals of instructing;
2. Knowledge of the technical subject areas;
3. Knowledge of the flight instructor's responsibilities concerning the pilot certification process;
4. Knowledge of the flight instructor's responsibilities concerning logbook entries and pilot certificate endorsements;
5. Ability to demonstrate the procedures and maneuvers selected by the examiner to the instrument instructor pilot skill level while giving effective instruction;
6. Competence in teaching the procedures and maneuvers selected by the examiner;
7. Competence in describing, recognizing, analyzing, and correcting common errors simulated by the examiner; and
8. Knowledge of the development and effective use of a course of training, a syllabus, and a lesson plan, including scenario-based training and collaborative assessment (learner centered grading).

Unsatisfactory Performance

If, in the judgment of the examiner, the applicant does not meet the standards of performance of any TASK performed, the associated AREA OF OPERATION is failed and therefore, the practical test is failed. The examiner or applicant may discontinue the test at any time when the failure of an AREA OF OPERATION makes the applicant ineligible for the certificate or rating sought. ***The test may be continued ONLY with the consent of the applicant.*** If the test is discontinued, the applicant is entitled to credit for only those AREAS OF OPERATION and TASKS satisfactorily performed; however, during the retest and at the discretion of the examiner, any TASK may be re-evaluated, including those previously passed. Specific reasons for disqualification are:

1. Failure to perform a procedure or maneuver to the instrument pilot skill level while giving effective flight instruction;
2. Failure to provide an effective instructional explanation while demonstrating a procedure or maneuver (explanation during the demonstration must be clear, concise, technically accurate, and complete with no prompting from the examiner);
3. Any action or lack of action by the applicant which requires corrective intervention by the examiner to maintain safe flight; and
4. Failure to use proper and effective visual scanning techniques to clear the area before and while performing maneuvers.
5. Failure to incorporate SRM principles throughout the practical test.

When a notice of disapproval is issued, the examiner shall record the applicant's unsatisfactory performance in terms of AREAS OF OPERATION.

Letter of Discontinuance

When a practical test is discontinued for reasons other than unsatisfactory performance (e.g., equipment failure, weather, or illness) FAA Form 8710-1, Airman Certificate and/or Rating Application, and, if applicable, the Airman Knowledge Test Report, shall be returned to the applicant. The examiner at that time shall prepare, sign, and issue a Letter of Discontinuance to the applicant. The Letter of Discontinuance should identify the AREAS OF OPERATION of the practical test that were successfully completed. The applicant shall be advised that the Letter of Discontinuance shall be presented to the examiner when the practical test is resumed, and made part of the certification file.

Single-Pilot Resource Management

The examiner shall evaluate the applicant's ability throughout the practical test to use good aeronautical decision-making procedures in order to evaluate risks. The evaluation will be recorded on the Judgment Assessment Matrix (see Appendix 3). The examiner shall accomplish this requirement by developing a scenario that incorporates as many TASKS as possible to evaluate the applicant's risk management in making safe aeronautical decisions. For example, the examiner may develop a scenario that incorporates weather decisions and performance planning.

The applicant's ability to utilize all the assets available in making a risk analysis to determine the safest course of action is essential for satisfactory performance. The scenario should be realistic and within the capabilities of the aircraft used for the practical test.

Single Pilot Resource Management (SRM) is defined as the art and science of managing all the resources (both on-board the aircraft and from outside sources) available to a single-pilot (prior and during flight) to ensure that the successful outcome of the flight is never in doubt. Single-Pilot Resource Management available resources can include human resources, hardware, and information. Human resources "...includes all other groups routinely working with the pilot who are involved in decisions that are required to operate a flight safely. These groups include, but are not limited to: dispatchers, weather briefers, maintenance personnel, and air traffic controllers." Single Pilot Resource Management is a set of skill competencies that must be evident in all TASKS in this practical test standard as applied to single-pilot operation.

The following six items are areas of SRM.

1. Aeronautical Decision Making

REFERENCES: FAA-H-8083-25, AC 60-22, FAA-H-8083-15.

Objective. To determine the applicant exhibits sound aeronautical decision making during the planning and execution of the planned flight. The applicant should:

1. Use a sound decision-making process, such as the DECIDE model, 3P model, or similar process when making critical decisions that will have an effect on the outcome of the flight. The applicant should be able to explain the factors and alternative courses of action that were considered while making the decision.
2. Recognize and explain any hazardous attitudes that may have influenced any decision.
3. Determine and execute an appropriate course of action to handle any situation that arises that may cause a change in the original flight plan, in such a way that leads to a safe and successful conclusion of the flight.
4. Explain how the elements of risk management, CFIT awareness, overall situational awareness, use of automation, and task management influenced the decisions made and the resulting course of action.

2. Risk Management

REFERENCES: FAA-H-8083-25; FITS document: Managing Risk through Scenario Based Training, Single Pilot Resource Management, and Learner Centered Grading.

Objective. To determine the applicant can utilize risk management tools and models to assess the potential risk associated with the planned flight during preflight planning and while in flight. The applicant should:

1. Explain the four fundamental risk elements associated with the flight being conducted in the given scenario and how each one was assessed.
2. Use a tool, such as the PAVE checklist, to help assess the four risk elements
3. Use a personal checklist, such as the I'MSAFE checklist, to determine personal risks.
4. Use weather reports and forecasts to determine weather risks associated with the flight.
5. Explain how to recognize risks and how mitigate those risks throughout the flight.
6. Use the 5P model to assess the risks associated with each of the five factors.

3. **Task Management**

REFERENCE: FAA-H-8083-15.

Objective. To determine the applicant can prioritize the various tasks associated with the planning and execution of the flight. The applicant should:

1. Explain how to prioritize tasks in such a way to minimize distractions from flying the aircraft.
2. Complete all tasks in a timely manner considering the phase of flight without causing a distraction from flying.
3. Execute all checklists and procedures in a manner that does not increase workload at critical times, such as intercepting the final approach course.

4. **Situational Awareness**

REFERENCES: FAA-H-8083-25, FAA-H-8083-15.

Objective. To determine the applicant can maintain situational awareness during all phases of the flight. The applicant should:

1. Explain the concept of situational awareness and associated factors.
2. Explain the dangers associated with becoming fixated on a particular problem to the exclusion of other aspects of the flight.
3. State the current situation at any time during the flight in such a way that displays an accurate assessment of the current and future status of the flight, including weather, terrain, traffic, ATC situation, fuel status, and aircraft status.
4. Uses the navigation displays, traffic displays, terrain displays, weather displays, and other features of the aircraft to maintain a complete and accurate awareness of the current situation and any reasonably anticipated changes that may occur.

5. Controlled Flight Into Terrain Awareness

REFERENCE: Controlled Flight Into Terrain Training Aid website: http://www.faa.gov/training_testing/training/media/cfit/volume1/titlepg.pdf

Objective. To determine the applicant can accurately assess risks associated with terrain and obstacles, maintain accurate awareness of terrain and obstacles, and can use appropriate techniques and procedures to avoid controlled flight into terrain or obstacles by using all resources available. The applicant should:

1. Use current charts and procedures during the planning of the flight to ensure the intended flightpath avoids terrain and obstacles.
2. Be aware of potential terrain and obstacle hazards along the intended route.
3. Explain the terrain display, such as TAWS or display installed in the aircraft.
4. Use the terrain display, such as TAWS or display installed in the aircraft, for navigation, to maintain situational awareness, and to avoid terrain and obstacles.
5. Plan departures and arrivals to avoid terrain and obstacles.
6. Alter flight as necessary to avoid terrain.
7. Plan any course diversion, for whatever reason, in a way that ensures proper terrain and obstruction clearance to the new destination.
8. Explain and understand aircraft performance limitations associated with CFIT accidents.

6. Automation Management

REFERENCE: FAA-H-8083-15.

Objective. To determine the applicant can effectively use the automation features of the aircraft, including autopilot and flight management systems, in such a way to manage workload and can remain aware of the current and anticipated modes and status of the automation. The applicant must:

1. Explain how to recognize the current mode of operation of the autopilot/FMS.
2. Explain how to recognize anticipated and unanticipated mode or status changes of the autopilot/FMS.
3. State at any time during the flight the current mode or status and what the next anticipated mode or status will be.
4. Use the autopilot/FMS to reduce workload as appropriate for the phase of flight, during emergency or abnormal operations.
5. Recognize unanticipated mode changes in a timely manner and promptly return the automation to the correct mode.

Applicant's Use of Checklists

Throughout the practical test, the applicant is evaluated on the use of an appropriate checklist. Proper use is dependent on the specific TASK being evaluated. The situation may be such that the use of the checklist, while accomplishing elements of an Objective, would be either unsafe or impracticable, especially in a single-pilot operation. In this case, a review of the checklist after the elements have been accomplished would be appropriate. Division of attention and proper visual scanning should be considered when using a checklist.

Use of Distractions During Practical Tests

Numerous studies indicate that many accidents have occurred when the pilot has been distracted during critical phases of flight. To evaluate the pilot's ability to utilize proper control technique while dividing attention both inside and/or outside the cockpit, the examiner shall cause a realistic distraction during the flight portion of the practical test to evaluate the applicant's ability to divide attention while maintaining safe flight.

Positive Exchange of Flight Controls

During flight, there must always be a clear understanding between the pilots of who has control of the aircraft. Prior to flight, a briefing should be conducted that includes the procedure for the exchange of flight controls. Some operators have established a two-step procedure for exchange of flight controls. A popular three-step process in the exchange of flight controls between pilots is explained below. Any safe procedure agreed to by the applicant and the examiner is acceptable.

When one pilot wishes to give the other pilot control of the aircraft, he or she will say, "You have the flight controls." The other pilot acknowledges immediately by saying, "I have the flight controls." The first pilot again says, "You have the flight controls." When control is returned to the first pilot, follow the same procedure. A visual check is recommended to verify that the exchange has occurred. There should never be any doubt as to who is flying the aircraft.

Emphasis on Attitude Instrument Flying and Partial Panel Skills

The FAA is concerned about numerous fatal accidents involving spatial disorientation of instrument rated pilots who have attempted to control and maneuver their aircraft in clouds with inoperative primary flight instruments (gyroscopic heading and/or attitude indicators) or loss of the primary electric flight instruments display.

The FAA has stressed that it is imperative for instrument pilots to acquire and maintain adequate instrument skills and that they be capable of performing instrument flight with the use of the backup systems installed in the aircraft. Many light aircraft operated in IMC are not equipped with dual, independent gyroscopic heading and/or attitude indicators and in many cases are equipped with only a single vacuum source. Technically advanced aircraft may be equipped with backup flight instruments or an additional electronic flight display that is not located directly in front of the pilot.

FAA-S-8081-4, Instrument Rating Practical Test Standards, and FAA-S-8081-9, Flight Instructor—Instrument Practical Test Standards, place increased emphasis on and require the demonstration of a nonprecision instrument approach without the use of the primary flight instruments or electronic flight instrument display. This practical test book, FAA-S-8081-9, emphasizes this area from an instructional standpoint.

AREA OF OPERATION VI requires the applicant to demonstrate the ability to teach basic instrument flight TASKS under both full panel and reference to backup primary flight instruments/electronic flight instrument displays. These maneuvers are described in detail in FAA-H-8083-15, Instrument Flying Handbook. Examiners should determine that the applicant demonstrates and fully understands either the PRIMARY and SUPPORTING or the CONTROL and PERFORMANCE CONCEPT method of attitude instrument flying. Both attitude instrument flying methods are described in FAA-H-8083-15, Instrument Flying Handbook. The TASKS require the applicant to exhibit instructional knowledge of instrument flying techniques and procedures and to demonstrate the ability to teach basic instrument maneuvers with both full panel and partial panel or reference to backup primary flight instruments/electronic flight instrument displays.

Change 2 (4/18/2014)

ADDITION OF AN INSTRUMENT INSTRUCTOR RATING TO A FLIGHT INSTRUCTOR CERTIFICATE

AREA OF OPERATION	FLIGHT INSTRUCTOR CERTIFICATE AND RATING HELD		
	AP	RTR	IA or H
I	N	N	N
II	A & C	A & C	C
III	B & C	B & C	C
IV	N	N	N
V	Y	Y	N
VI	Y	Y	Y
VII	Y	Y	N
VIII	Y	Y	* A or B
IX	Y	Y	Y
X	Y	Y	Y

LEGEND
AP   Airplane
RTR   Helicopter/Gyroplane
IA or H   Instrument Airplane or Helicopter

NOTE: N indicates that the AREA OF OPERATION is not required. Y indicates that the AREA OF OPERATION is to be performed or based on the note in the AREA OF OPERATION. If a TASK (or TASKS) is listed for an AREA OF OPERATION, that TASK (or TASKS) is mandatory.

* Combine with C, D, or E.

RENEWAL OR REINSTATEMENT OF A FLIGHT INSTRUCTOR

REQUIRED AREAS OF OPERATION	NUMBER OF TASKS
II	TASK "D" and one other TASK
III	1
IV	1
V	1
VI	2
VII	1
VIII	A or B combined with TASK C, D, or E
IX	1

The Renewal or reinstatement of one rating on a Flight Instructor Certificate renews or reinstates all privileges existing on the certificate. (14 CFR part 61, sections 61.197 and 61.199)

APPLICANT'S PRACTICAL TEST CHECKLIST

Flight Instructor—Instrument

APPOINTMENT WITH INSPECTOR OR EXAMINER:

NAME _____

DATE/TIME _____

- ☐ View-limiting Device
- ☐ Aircraft Documents: Airworthiness Certificate, Registration Certificate, and Operating Limitations
- ☐ Aircraft Maintenance Records: Logbook Record of Airworthiness Inspections and AD Compliance
- ☐ Pilot's Operating Handbook and FAA-Approved Flight Manual

PERSONAL EQUIPMENT

- ☐ Practical Test Standards
- ☐ Lesson Plan Library
- ☐ Current Aeronautical Charts
- ☐ Computer and Plotter
- ☐ Flight Plan and Flight Log Forms
- ☐ Current AIM, Airport Facility Directory, and Appropriate Publications

PERSONAL RECORDS

- ☐ Identification—Photo/Signature ID
- ☐ Pilot Certificate
- ☐ Current and Appropriate Medical Certificate
- ☐ Completed FAA Form 8710-1, Airman Certificate and/or Rating Application
- ☐ Airman Knowledge Test Report
- ☐ Pilot Logbook with Appropriate Instructor Endorsements
- ☐ FAA Form 8060-5, Notice of Disapproval (if applicable)
- ☐ Approved School Graduation Certificate (if applicable)
- ☐ Examiner's Fee (if applicable)

EXAMINER'S PRACTICAL TEST CHECKLIST
Flight Instructor—Instrument

APPLICANT'S NAME _____

LOCATION _____

DATE/TIME _____

I. FUNDAMENTALS OF INSTRUCTING

- ☐ A. The Learning Process
- ☐ B. Human Behavior and Effective Communication
- ☐ C. The Teaching Process
- ☐ D. Teaching Methods
- ☐ E. Critique and Evaluation
- ☐ F. Flight Instructor Characteristics and Responsibilities
- ☐ G. Planning Instructional Activity

II. TECHNICAL SUBJECT AREAS

- ☐ A. Aircraft Flight Instruments and Navigation Equipment
- ☐ B. Aeromedical Factors
- ☐ C. Regulations and Publications Related to IFR Operations
- ☐ D. Logbook Entries Related to Instrument Instruction

III. PREFLIGHT PREPARATION

- ☐ A. Weather Information
- ☐ B. Cross-Country Flight Planning
- ☐ C. Instrument Cockpit Check

IV. PREFLIGHT LESSON ON A MANEUVER TO BE PERFORMED IN FLIGHT

- ☐ A. Maneuver Lesson

V. AIR TRAFFIC CONTROL CLEARANCES AND PROCEDURES

- ☐ A. Air Traffic Control Clearances
- ☐ B. Compliance with Departure, En Route, and Arrival Procedures and Clearances

VI. FLIGHT BY REFERENCE TO INSTRUMENTS

- ☐ **A.** Straight-and-Level Flight
- ☐ **B.** Turns
- ☐ **C.** Change of Airspeed in Straight-and-Level and Turning Flight
- ☐ **D.** Constant Airspeed Climbs and Descents
- ☐ **E.** Constant Rate Climbs and Descents
- ☐ **F.** Timed Turns to Magnetic Compass Headings
- ☐ **G.** Steep Turns
- ☐ **H.** Recovery from Unusual Flight Attitudes

VII. NAVIGATION SYSTEMS

- ☐ **A.** Intercepting and Tracking Navigational Systems and DME Arcs
- ☐ **B.** Holding Procedures

VIII. INSTRUMENT APPROACH PROCEDURES

- ☐ **A.** Nonpecision Instrument Approach
- ☐ **B.** Precision Instrument Approach
- ☐ **C.** Missed Approach
- ☐ **D.** Circling Approach (Airplane)
- ☐ **E.** Landing From a Straight-In Approach

IX. EMERGENCY OPERATIONS

- ☐ **A.** Loss of Communications
- ☐ **B.** Loss of Gyro Attitude and Heading Indicators
- ☐ **C.** Engine Failure During Straight-and-Level Flight and Turns
- ☐ **D.** Instrument Approach—One Engine Inoperative

X. POSTFLIGHT PROCEDURES

- ☐ **A.** Checking Instruments and Equipment

I. AREA OF OPERATION: FUNDAMENTALS OF INSTRUCTING

NOTE: The examiner shall select at least TASK E, F, and G and one other task.

A. TASK: LEARNING PROCESS

REFERENCE: FAA-H-8083-9.

Objective. To determine that the applicant exhibits instructional knowledge of the elements of the learning process by describing:

1. Learning theories.
2. Characteristics of learning.
3. Principles of learning.
4. Levels of learning.
5. Learning physical skills.
6. Memory.
7. Transfer of learning.

B. TASK: HUMAN BEHAVIOR AND EFFECTIVE COMMUNICATION

REFERENCE: FAA-H-8083-9.

Objective. To determine that the applicant exhibits instructional knowledge of the elements of human behavior and effective communication as it applies to the teaching/learning process by describing:

1. Human behavior—

    a. control of human behavior.
    b. human needs.
    c. defense mechanisms.
    d. the flight instructor as a practical psychologist.

2. Effective communication

    a. basic elements of communication.
    b. barriers of effective communication.
    c. developing communication skills.

C. TASK: TEACHING PROCESS

REFERENCE: FAA-H-8083-9.

Objective. To determine that the applicant exhibits instructional knowledge of the elements of the teaching process by describing:

1. Preparation of a lesson for a ground or flight instructional period.
2. Presentation methods.
3. Application, by the student, of the material or procedure that was presented.
4. Review and evaluation of student performance.
5. Problem-based learning.

D. TASK: TEACHING METHODS

REFERENCE: FAA-H-8083-9.

Objective. To determine that the applicant exhibits instructional knowledge of the elements of teaching methods by describing:

1. Material organization.
2. The lecture method.
3. The cooperative or group learning method.
4. The guided discussion method.
5. The demonstration-performance method.
6. Computer-based training method.
7. Scenario-based training method.

E. TASK: CRITIQUE AND EVALUATION

REFERENCE: FAA-H-8083-9.

Objective. To determine that the applicant exhibits instructional knowledge of the elements of critique and evaluation by explaining:

1. Critique—

    a. purpose and characteristics of an effective critique.
    b. methods and ground rules for a critique.

2. Evaluation—

    a. characteristics of effective oral questions and what types to avoid.
    b. responses to student questions.
    c. characteristics and development of effective written test.
    d. characteristics and uses of performance tests, specifically, the FAA Practical Test Standards.
    e. collaborative assessment (or learner-centered grading (LCG)).

F. TASK: FLIGHT INSTRUCTOR CHARACTERISTICS AND RESPONSIBILITIES

REFERENCE: FAA-H-8083-9.

Objective. To determine that the applicant exhibits instructional knowledge of the elements of instructor responsibilities and professionalism by describing:

1. Aviation instructor responsibilities in—

    a. providing adequate instruction.
    b. establishing standards of performance.
    c. emphasizing the positive.

2. Flight instructor responsibilities in—

    a. providing student pilot evaluation and supervision.
    b. preparing practical test recommendations and endorsements.
    c. determining requirements for conducting additional training and endorsement requirements.

3. Professionalism as an instructor by—

    a. explaining important personal characteristics.
    b. describing methods to minimize student frustration.

G. TASK: PLANNING INSTRUCTIONAL ACTIVITY

REFERENCE: FAA-H-8083-9.

Objective. To determine that the applicant exhibits instructional knowledge of the elements of planning instructional activity by describing:

1. Developing objectives and standards for a course of training.
2. Theory of building blocks of learning.
3. Requirements for developing a training syllabus.
4. Purpose and characteristics of a lesson plan.
5. How a scenario-based lesson is developed.

II. AREA OF OPERATION: TECHNICAL SUBJECT AREAS

NOTE: The examiner shall select TASKS A and D and at least one other TASK.

A. TASK: AIRCRAFT FLIGHT INSTRUMENTS AND NAVIGATION EQUIPMENT

REFERENCES: FAA-H-8083-15, FAA-S-8081-4.

Objective. To determine that the applicant exhibits instructional knowledge of aircraft:

1. Flight instrument systems and their operating characteristics to include—

    a. pitot-static system.
    b. attitude indicator.
    c. heading indicator/horizontal situation indicator/radio magnetic indicator.
    d. magnetic compass.
    e. turn-and-slip indicator/turn coordinator.
    f. electrical system.
    g. vacuum system.
    h. electronic engine instrument display.
    i. primary flight display, if installed.

2. Navigation equipment and their operating characteristics to include—

    a. VHF omnirange (VOR).
    b. distance measuring equipment (DME).
    c. instrument landing system (ILS)
    d. marker beacon receiver/indicators.
    e. automatic direction finder (ADF).
    f. transponder/altitude encoding.
    g. electronic flight instrument display.
    h. global positioning system (GPS)
    i. automatic pilot.
    j. flight management system (FMS).
    k. multifunction display, if installed.

3. Anti-ice/deicing and weather detection equipment and their operating characteristics to include—

    a. airframe.
    b. propeller or rotor.
    c. air intake.
    d. fuel system.
    e. pitot-static system.
    f. radar/lightning detection system.
    g. other inflight weather systems.

B. TASK: AEROMEDICAL FACTORS

REFERENCES: FAA-H-8083-25; AIM.

Objective. To determine that the applicant exhibits instructional knowledge of the elements related to aeromedical factors by describing the effects, corrective action, and safety considerations of:

1. Hypoxia.
2. Hyperventilation.
3. Middle ear and sinus problems.
4. Spatial disorientation.
5. Motion sickness.
6. Alcohol and drugs.
7. Carbon monoxide poisoning.
8. Evolved gases from scuba diving.
9. Stress and fatigue.

C. TASK: REGULATIONS AND PUBLICATIONS RELATED TO IFR OPERATIONS

REFERENCES: 14 CFR parts 61, 71, 91, 95, and 97; FAA-H-8083-15; AIM.

Objective. To determine that the applicant exhibits instructional knowledge of the elements related to regulations and publications, (related to instrument flight and instrument flight instruction) their purpose, general content, availability, and method of revision by describing:

1. 14 CFR parts 61, 71, 91, 95, and 97.
2. FAA-H-8083-15, Instrument Flying Handbook.
3. Aeronautical Information Manual.
4. Practical Test Standards.
5. Airport Facility Directory.
6. Standard Instrument Departures/Terminal Arrivals.
7. En Route Charts.
8. Standard Instrument Approach Procedure Charts.

D. TASK: LOGBOOK ENTRIES RELATED TO INSTRUMENT INSTRUCTION

REFERENCES: 14 CFR part 61; AC 61-65; AC 61-98.

Objective. To determine that the applicant exhibits instructional knowledge of logbook entries related to instrument instruction by describing:

1. Logbook entries or training records for instrument flight/ instrument flight instruction or ground instruction given.
2. Preparation of a recommendation for an instrument rating practical test, including appropriate logbook entry.
3. Required endorsement of a pilot logbook for satisfactory completion of an instrument proficiency check.
4. Required flight instructor records.

III. AREA OF OPERATION: PREFLIGHT PREPARATION

NOTE: The examiner shall select at least one TASK.

A. TASK: WEATHER INFORMATION

NOTE: If the current weather reports, forecasts, or other pertinent information is not available, or if the current weather is not appropriate for the practical test scenario, then weather reports, forecasts, and other pertinent information shall be simulated by the examiner in a manner to adequately measure the applicant's competence.

REFERENCES: AC 00-6, AC 00-45; FAA-S-8081-4; AIM.

Objective. To determine that the applicant exhibits instructional knowledge related to IFR weather information.

1. Sources of weather—

    a. AWOS, ASOS, and ATIS reports.
    b. PATWAS and TIBS.
    c. TWEB.

2. Weather reports and charts—

    a. METAR, TAF, FA, and radar reports.
    b. inflight weather advisories.
    c. surface analysis, weather depiction, and radar summary charts.
    d. significant weather prognostic charts.
    e. winds and temperatures aloft charts.
    f. pilot weather reports (PIREPS).
    g. freezing level charts.
    h. stability charts.
    i. severe weather outlook charts.
    j. SIGMETS and AIRMETS.

B. TASK: CROSS-COUNTRY FLIGHT PLANNING

REFERENCES: 14 CFR part 91; FAA-H-8083-15, FAA-S-8081-4; AIM.

Objective. To determine that the applicant exhibits instructional knowledge of cross-country flight planning by describing the:

1. Regulatory requirements for instrument flight within various types of airspace.
2. Computation of estimated time en route and total fuel requirement for an IFR cross-country flight.
3. Selection and correct interpretation of the current and applicable en route charts, RNAV, DPs, STARs, and standard instrument approach procedure charts (IAP).
4. Procurement and interpretation of the applicable NOTAM information.
5. Completes and files an IFR flight plan that accurately reflects the conditions of the proposed flight. (Does not have to be filed with ATC.)
6. Demonstrates adequate knowledge of GPS and RAIM capability, when aircraft is so equipped.
7. Demonstrates the ability to recognize wing contamination due to airframe icing.
8. Demonstrates adequate knowledge of the adverse effects of airframe icing during landing phases of flight and corrective actions: pretakeoff, takeoff, and cruise.
9. Demonstrates familiarity with any icing procedures and/or information published by the manufacturer that is specific to the aircraft used on the practical test.

C. TASK: INSTRUMENT COCKPIT CHECK

REFERENCES: 14 CFR part 91; FAA-H-8083-15, FAA-S-8081-4.

Objective. To determine that the applicant exhibits instructional knowledge of an instrument cockpit check by describing the reasons for the check and the detection of defects that could affect safe instrument flight. The check shall include:

1. Communications equipment.
2. Navigation equipment.
3. Magnetic compass.
4. Heading indicator/horizontal situation indicator/remote magnetic indicator.
5. Attitude indicator.
6. Altimeter.
7. Turn-and-slip indicator/turn coordinator.
8. Vertical-speed indicator.
9. Airspeed indicator.
10. Outside air temperature.
11. Clock.

12. Pilot heat.
13. Electronic flight instrument display.
14. Traffic awareness/warning/avoidance system.
15. Terrain awareness/warning/alert system.
16. Flight management system (FMS).
17. Automatic pilot.

IV. AREA OF OPERATION: PREFLIGHT LESSON ON A MANEUVER TO BE PERFORMED IN FLIGHT

NOTE: The examiner shall select at least one maneuver from AREAS OF OPERATION VI through IX and ask the applicant to present a preflight lesson on the selected maneuver as the lesson would be taught to a student. Previously developed lesson plans from the applicant's library may be used.

A. TASK: MANEUVER LESSON

REFERENCES: FAA-H-8083-9, FAA-H-8083-15; FAA-S-8081-4.

Objective. To determine that the applicant exhibits instructional knowledge of the selected maneuver by:

1. Using a lesson plan that includes all essential items to make an effective and organized presentation.
2. Stating the objective.
3. Giving an accurate, comprehensive oral description of the maneuver, including the elements and associated common errors.
4. Using instructional aids, as appropriate.
5. Describing the recognition, analysis, and correction of common errors.

V. AREA OF OPERATION: AIR TRAFFIC CONTROL CLEARANCES AND PROCEDURES

NOTE: The examiner shall select at least one TASK.

A. TASK: AIR TRAFFIC CONTROL CLEARANCES

REFERENCES: 14 CFR part 91; FAA-H-8083-15; FAA-S-8081-4.

Objective. To determine that the applicant exhibits instructional knowledge of air traffic control clearances by describing:

1. Pilot and controller responsibilities to include tower, en route control, and clearance void times.
2. Correct and timely copying of an ATC clearance.
3. Ability to comply with the clearance.
4. Correct and timely read-back of an ATC clearance, using standard phraseology.
5. Correct interpretation of an ATC clearance and, when necessary, request for clarification, verification, or change.
6. Setting of communication and navigation frequencies in compliance with an ATC clearance.

B. TASK: COMPLIANCE WITH DEPARTURE, EN ROUTE, AND ARRIVAL PROCEDURES AND CLEARANCES

REFERENCES: 14 CFR part 91; FAA-H-8083-15; FAA-S-8081-4; AIM.

Objective. To determine that the applicant exhibits instructional knowledge of the elements related to compliance with departure, en route, and arrival procedures and clearances by describing:

1. Selection and use of current and appropriate navigation publications.
2. Pilot and controller responsibilities with regard to DPs, En Route Low and High Altitude Charts, and STARs.
3. Selection and use of appropriate communications frequencies.
4. Selection and identification of the navigation aids.
5. Accomplishment of the appropriate checklist items.
6. Pilot's responsibility for compliance with vectors and also altitude, airspeed, climb, descent, and airspace restrictions.
7. Pilot's responsibility for the interception of courses, radials, and bearings appropriate to the procedure, route, or clearance.
8. Procedures to be used in the event of two-way communications failure.
9. The uses of the multifunction display and other graphical navigational displays, if installed, to monitor position track, wind drift, and other parameters to maintain situational awareness and desired flightpath.

VI. AREA OF OPERATION: FLIGHT BY REFERENCE TO INSTRUMENTS

NOTE: The examiner shall select TASK H and at least one other TASK. The applicant shall select either the primary and supporting or the control and performance method for teaching this AREA OF OPERATION.

A. TASK: STRAIGHT-AND-LEVEL FLIGHT

REFERENCES: FAA-H-8083-9, FAA-H-8083-15; FAA-S-8081-4.

Objective. To determine that the applicant:

1. Exhibits instructional knowledge of teaching straight-and-level flight by describing—

    a. the relationship of pitch, bank, and power in straight-and-level flight.
    b. procedure using full panel and partial panel
    c. coordination of controls and trim.

2. Exhibits instructional knowledge of common errors related to straight-and-level flight by describing—

    a. slow or improper cross-check during straight-and-level flight.
    b. improper power control.
    c. failure to make smooth, precise corrections, as required.
    d. uncoordinated use of controls.
    e. improper trim control.

3. Demonstrates and simultaneously explains straight-and-level flight from an instructional standpoint.
4. Analyzes and corrects simulated common errors related to straight-and-level flight.

B. TASK: TURNS

REFERENCES: FAA-H-8083-9, FAA-H-8083-15; FAA-S-8081-4.

Objective. To determine that the applicant:

1. Exhibits instructional knowledge of teaching turns by describing—

    a. the relationship of true airspeed and angle of bank to a standard rate turn.
    b. technique and procedure using full panel and partial panel for entry and recovery of a constant rate turn, including the performance of a half-standard rate turn.
    c. coordination of controls and trim.

2. Exhibits instructional knowledge of common errors related to turns by describing—

    a. improper cross-check procedures.
    b. improper bank control during roll-in and roll-out.
    c. failure to make smooth, precise corrections, as required.
    d. uncoordinated use of controls.
    e. improper trim technique.

3. Demonstrates and simultaneously explains turns from an instructional standpoint.
4. Analyzes and corrects simulated common errors related to turns.

C. TASK: CHANGE OF AIRSPEED IN STRAIGHT-AND-LEVEL AND TURNING FLIGHT

REFERENCES: FAA-H-8083-9, FAA-H-8083-15; FAA-S-8081-4.

Objective. To determine that the applicant:

1. Exhibits instructional knowledge of teaching change of airspeed in straight-and-level flight and turns by describing—

    a. procedure using full panel and partial panel for maintaining altitude and changing airspeed in straight-and-level and turning flight.
    b. coordination of controls and trim technique.

2. Exhibits instructional knowledge of common errors related to changes of airspeed in straight-and-level and turning flight by describing—

    a. slow or improper cross-check during straight-and-level flight and turns.
    b. improper power control.
    c. failure to make smooth, precise corrections, as required.
    d. uncoordinated use of controls.
    e. improper trim technique.

3. Demonstrates and simultaneously explains changes of airspeed in straight-and-level and turning flight from an instructional standpoint.
4. Analyzes and corrects simulated common errors related to changes of airspeed in straight-and-level and turning flight.

D. TASK: CONSTANT AIRSPEED CLIMBS AND DESCENTS

REFERENCES: FAA-H-8083-9, FAA-H-8083-15; FAA-S-8081-4.

Objective. To determine that the applicant:

1. Exhibits instructional knowledge of constant airspeed climbs and descents by describing—

    a. procedure using full panel and partial panel for an entry into a straight climb or climbing turn, from either cruising or climbing airspeed.
    b. a stabilized straight climb or climbing turn.
    c. a level-off from a straight climb or climbing turn, at either cruising or climbing airspeed.
    d. procedure using full panel and partial panel for an entry into a straight descent or descending turn from either cruising or descending airspeed.
    e. a stabilized straight descent or descending turn.
    f. a level-off from a straight descent or descending turn, at either cruising or descending airspeed.

2. Exhibits instructional knowledge of common errors related to constant airspeed climbs and descents by describing—

    a. failure to use a proper power setting and pitch attitude.
    b. improper correction of vertical rate, airspeed, heading, or rate-of-turn errors.
    c. uncoordinated use of controls.
    d. improper trim control.

3. Demonstrates and simultaneously explains a constant airspeed climb and a constant airspeed descent from an instructional standpoint.
4. Analyzes and corrects simulated common errors related to constant airspeed climbs and descents.

E. TASK: CONSTANT RATE CLIMBS AND DESCENTS

REFERENCES: FAA-H-8083-9, FAA-H-8083-15; FAA-S-8081-4.

Objective. To determine that the applicant:

1. Exhibits instructional knowledge of constant rate climbs and descents by describing—

   a. procedure using full panel and partial panel for an entry into a constant rate climb or descent.
   b. a stabilized constant rate straight climb or climbing turn, using the vertical speed indicator.
   c. a level-off from a constant rate straight climb or climbing turn.
   d. an entry into a constant rate straight descent or descending turn.
   e. a stabilized constant rate straight descent or descending turn using the vertical speed indicator.
   f. level-off from a constant rate straight descent or descending turn.

2. Exhibits instructional knowledge of common errors related to constant rate climbs and descents by describing—

   a. failure to use a proper power setting and pitch attitude.
   b. improper correction of vertical rate, airspeed, heading, or rate-of-turn errors.
   c. uncoordinated use of controls.
   d. improper trim control.

3. Demonstrates and simultaneously explains a constant rate climb and a constant rate descent from an instructional standpoint.
4. Analyzes and corrects simulated common errors related to constant rate climbs and descents.

F. TASK: TIMED TURNS TO MAGNETIC COMPASS HEADINGS

REFERENCES: FAA-H-8083-9, FAA-H-8083-15; FAA-S-8081-4.

Objective. To determine that the applicant:

1. Exhibits instructional knowledge of timed turns to magnetic compass headings by describing—

   a. operating characteristics and errors of the magnetic compass.
   b. calibration of the miniature aircraft of the turn coordinator[2], both right and left, using full panel and the clock.
   c. procedures using full panel and partial panel performing compass turns to a specified heading.

2. Exhibits instructional knowledge of common errors related to timed turns to magnetic compass headings by describing—

   a. incorrect calibration procedures.
   b. improper timing.
   c. uncoordinated use of controls.
   d. improper trim control.

3. Demonstrates and simultaneously explains timed turns to magnetic compass headings from an instructional standpoint.
4. Analyzes and corrects simulated common errors related to timed turns to magnetic compass headings.

---

[2] If the aircraft used for the practical test has a turn needle, substitute turn needle for miniature aircraft of turn coordinator.

G. TASK: STEEP TURNS

REFERENCES: FAA-H-8083-9, FAA-H-8083-15; FAA-S-8081-4.

Objective. To determine that the applicant:

1. Exhibits instructional knowledge of steep turns by describing—

    a. procedure using full panel and partial panel for entry and recovery of a steep turn.
    b. the need for a proper instrument cross-check.
    c. roll-in/roll-out procedure.
    d. coordination of control and trim.

2. Exhibits instructional knowledge of common errors related to steep turns by describing—

    a. failure to recognize and make proper corrections for pitch, bank, or power errors.
    b. failure to compensate for precession of the horizon bar of the attitude indicator.
    c. uncoordinated use of controls.
    d. improper trim technique.

3. Demonstrates and simultaneously explains steep turns from an instructional standpoint.
4. Analyzes and corrects simulated common errors related to steep turns.

H. TASK: RECOVERY FROM UNUSUAL FLIGHT ATTITUDES

REFERENCES: FAA-H-8083-9, FAA-H-8083-15; FAA-S-8081-4.

Objective. To determine that the applicant:

1. Exhibits instructional knowledge of recovery from unusual flight attitudes by describing—

    a. conditions or situations which contribute to the development of unusual flight attitudes.
    b. procedure using full panel and partial panel for recovery from nose-high and nose-low unusual flight attitudes.

2. Exhibits instructional knowledge of common errors related to recovery from unusual flight attitudes by describing—

    a. incorrect interpretation of the flight instruments.
    b. inappropriate application of controls.

3. Demonstrates and simultaneously explains recovery from unusual flight attitudes, solely by reference to instruments, from an instructional standpoint.
4. Analyzes and corrects simulated common errors related to recovery from unusual flight attitudes.

VII. AREA OF OPERATION: NAVIGATION SYSTEMS

NOTE: The examiner shall select TASK A and B. If aircraft is not DME equipped, performance of DME arcs shall be tested orally.

A. TASK: INTERCEPTING AND TRACKING NAVIGATIONAL SYSTEMS AND DME ARCS

REFERENCES: 14 CFR part 91; FAA-H-8083-9, FAA-H-8083-15; FAA-S-8081-4; AIM.

Objective. To determine that the applicant:

1. Exhibits instructional knowledge of the elements of intercepting and tracking navigational systems and DME arcs by describing—

    a. tuning and identification of a navigational facility.
    b. setting of a selected course on the navigation selector or the correct identification of a selected bearing on the RMI.
    c. method for determining aircraft position relative to a facility.
    d. procedure for intercepting and maintaining a selected course.
    e. procedure for intercepting and maintaining a DME arc.
    f. procedure for intercepting a course or localizer from a DME arc.
    g. recognition of navigation facility or waypoint passage.
    h. recognition of navigation receiver or facility failure.

2. Exhibits instructional knowledge of common errors related to intercepting and tracking navigational systems and DME arcs by describing—

    a. incorrect tuning and identification procedures.
    b. failure to properly set the navigation selector on the course to be intercepted.
    c. failure to use proper procedures for course or DME arc interception and tracking.
    d. improper procedures for intercepting a course or localizer from a DME arc.

3. Demonstrates and simultaneously explains intercepting and tracking navigational systems and DME arcs from an instructional standpoint.
4. Analyzes and corrects simulated common errors related to intercepting and tracking navigational systems and DME arcs.
5. Exhibits instructional knowledge on the uses of the MFD and other graphical navigational displays, if installed, to monitor position in relation to the desired flightpath during holding.

B. TASK: HOLDING PROCEDURES

REFERENCES: 14 CFR part 91; FAA-H-8083-9, FAA-H-8083-15; FAA-S-8081-4; AIM.

Objective. To determine that the applicant:

1. Exhibits instructional knowledge of holding procedures by describing—

    a. setting of aircraft navigation equipment.
    b. requirement for establishing the appropriate holding airspeed for the aircraft and altitude.
    c. recognition of arrival at the holding fix and the prompt initiation of entry into the holding pattern.
    d. timing procedure.
    e. correction for wind drift.
    f. use of DME in a holding pattern.
    g. compliance with ATC reporting requirements.

2. Exhibits instructional knowledge of common errors related to holding procedures by describing—

    a. incorrect setting of aircraft navigation equipment.
    b. inappropriate altitude, airspeed, and bank control.
    c. improper timing.
    d. improper wind drift correction.
    e. failure to recognize holding fix passage.
    f. failure to comply with ATC instructions.

3. Demonstrates and simultaneously explains holding procedures from an instructional standpoint.
4. Analyzes and corrects simulated common errors related to holding procedures.
5. Exhibits instructional knowledge on the use of the MFD and other graphical navigational displays, if installed, to monitor position in relation to the desired flightpath during holding.

VIII. AREA OF OPERATION: INSTRUMENT APPROACH PROCEDURES

NOTE: The examiner shall select TASKS A and B, to be combined with TASK C, D, or E. At least one nonprecision approach procedure shall be accomplished without the use of the gyroscopic heading and attitude indicators under simulated instrument conditions. Circling approaches are not applicable to helicopters.

A. TASK: NONPRECISION INSTRUMENT APPROACH (NPA)

REFERENCES: 14 CFR part 91; FAA-H-8083-9, FAA-H-8083-15; FAA-S-8081-4; IAP; AIM.

Objective. To determine that the applicant:

1. Exhibits instructional knowledge of the elements of a nonprecision instrument approach by describing—

   a. selection of the appropriate instrument approach procedure chart.
   b. pertinent information on the selected instrument approach chart.
   c. radio communications with ATC and compliance with ATC clearances, instructions, and procedures.
   d. appropriate aircraft configuration, airspeed, and checklist items.
   e. selection, tuning, identification, and determination of operational status of ground and aircraft navigation equipment.
   f. adjustments applied to the published MDA and visibility criteria for the aircraft approach category.
   g. maintenance of altitude, airspeed, and track, where applicable.
   h. establishment and maintenance of an appropriate rate of descent during the final approach segment.
   i. factors that should be considered in determining whether:

      (1) the approach should be continued straight-in to a landing;
      (2) a circling approach to a landing should be made; or
      (3) a missed approach should be performed.

2. Exhibits instructional knowledge of common errors related to a nonprecision instrument approach by describing—

   a. failure to have essential knowledge of the information on the instrument approach chart.
   b. incorrect communications procedures or noncompliance with ATC clearances or instructions.

      c. failure to accomplish checklist items.
      d. faulty basic instrument flying technique.
      e. inappropriate descent below the MDA.

3. Demonstrates and simultaneously explains a nonprecision instrument approach from an instructional standpoint.
4. Analyzes and corrects simulated common errors related to a nonprecision instrument approach.
5. Exhibits instructional knowledge on the uses of the MFD and other graphical navigational displays, if installed, to monitor position, track, wind drift, and other parameters to maintain desired flightpath.

B. TASK: PRECISION INSTRUMENT APPROACH (PA)

REFERENCES: 14 CFR part 91; FAA-H-8083-9, FAA-H-8083-15; FAA-S-8081-4; IAP; AIM.

Objective. To determine that the applicant:

1. Exhibits instructional knowledge of a precision instrument approach by describing—

    a. selection of the appropriate instrument approach chart.
    b. pertinent information on the selected instrument approach chart.
    c. selection, tuning, identification, and determination of operational status of ground and aircraft navigation equipment.
    d. radio communications with ATC and compliance with ATC clearances, instructions, and procedures.
    e. appropriate aircraft configuration, airspeed, and checklist items.
    f. adjustments applied to the published DH/DA and visibility criteria for the aircraft approach category.
    g. maintenance of altitude, airspeed, and track, where applicable.
    h. establishment and maintenance of an appropriate rate of descent during the final approach segment.
    i. factors that should be considered in determining whether:

        (1) the approach should be continued straight-in to a landing;
        (2) a circling approach to a landing should be made; or
        (3) a missed approach should be performed.

2. Exhibits instructional knowledge of common errors related to a precision instrument approach by describing—

    a. failure to have essential knowledge of the information on the instrument approach procedure chart.
    b. incorrect communications procedures or noncompliance with ATC clearances.
    c. failure to accomplish checklist items.
    d. faulty basic instrument flying technique.
    e. inappropriate application of DH/DA.

3. Demonstrates and simultaneously explains a precision instrument approach from an instructional standpoint.
4. Analyzes and corrects simulated common errors related to a precision instrument approach.
5. Exhibits instructional knowledge on the uses of the MFD and other parameters to maintain desired flightpath.

C. TASK: MISSED APPROACH

REFERENCES: 14 CFR part 91; FAA-H-8083-9, FAA-H-8083-15; FAA-S-8081-4; IAP; AIM.

Objective. To determine that the applicant:

1. Exhibits instructional knowledge of a missed approach procedure by describing—

    a. pertinent information on the selected instrument approach chart.
    b. conditions requiring a missed approach.
    c. initiation of the missed approach, including the prompt application of power, establishment of a climb attitude, and reduction of drag.
    d. required report to ATC.
    e. compliance with the published or alternate missed approach procedure.
    f. notification of ATC if the aircraft is unable to comply with a clearance, instruction, restriction, or climb gradient.
    g. performance of recommended checklist items appropriate to the go-around procedure.
    h. importance of positive aircraft control.

2. Exhibits instructional knowledge of common errors related to a missed approach by describing—

    a. failure to have essential knowledge of the information on the instrument approach chart.
    b. failure to recognize conditions requiring a missed approach.
    c. failure to promptly initiate a missed approach.
    d. failure to make the required report to ATC.
    e. failure to comply with the missed approach procedure.
    f. faulty basic instrument flying technique.
    g. descent below the MDA prior to initiating a missed approach.

3. Demonstrates and simultaneously explains a missed approach from an instructional standpoint.
4. Analyzes and corrects simulated common errors related to a missed approach.
5. Exhibits instructional knowledge on the uses of the MFD and other graphical navigational displays, if installed, to monitor position and track to help navigate the missed approach.

D. TASK: CIRCLING APPROACH (AIRPLANE)

REFERENCES: 14 CFR part 91; FAA-H-8083-9, FAA-H-8083-15; FAA-S-8081-4; IAP; AIM.

Objective. To determine that the applicant:

1. Exhibits instructional knowledge of the elements of a circling approach by describing—

    a. selection of the appropriate circling approach maneuver considering the maneuvering capabilities of the aircraft.
    b. circling approach minimums on the selected instrument approach chart.
    c. compliance with advisories, clearance instructions, and/or restrictions.
    d. importance of flying a circling approach pattern that does not exceed the published visibility criteria.
    e. maintenance of an altitude no lower than the circling MDA until in a position from which a descent to a normal landing can be made.

2. Exhibits instructional knowledge of common errors related to a circling approach by describing—

    a. failure to have essential knowledge of the circling approach information on the instrument approach chart.
    b. failure to adhere to the published MDA and visibility criteria during the circling approach maneuver.
    c. inappropriate pilot technique during transition from the circling maneuver to the landing approach.

3. Demonstrates and simultaneously explains a circling approach from an instructional standpoint.
4. Analyzes and corrects simulated common errors related to a circling approach.

E. TASK: LANDING FROM A STRAIGHT-IN APPROACH

REFERENCES: 14 CFR part 91; FAA-H-8083-9, FAA-H-8083-15; FAA-S-8081-4; IAP; AIM.

Objective. To determine that the applicant:

1. Exhibits instructional knowledge of the elements related to landing from a straight-in approach by describing—

   a. effect of specific environmental, operational, and meteorological factors.
   b. transition to, and maintenance of, a visual flight condition.
   c. adherence to ATC advisories, such as NOTAMs, wind shear, wake turbulence, runway surface, and braking conditions.
   d. completion of appropriate checklist items.
   e. maintenance of positive aircraft control.

2. Exhibits instructional knowledge of common errors related to landing from a straight-in approach by describing—

   a. inappropriate division of attention during the transition from instrument to visual flight conditions.
   b. failure to complete required checklist items.
   c. failure to properly plan and perform the turn to final approach.
   d. improper technique for wind shear, wake turbulence, and crosswind.
   e. failure to maintain positive aircraft control throughout the complete landing maneuver.

3. Demonstrates and simultaneously explains a landing from a straight-in approach from an instructional standpoint.
4. Analyzes and corrects simulated common errors related to landing from a straight-in approach.

IX. AREA OF OPERATION: EMERGENCY OPERATIONS

NOTE: The examiner shall select at least one TASK. The examiner shall omit TASKS C and D unless the applicant furnishes a multiengine airplane for the practical test, then TASK C or D is mandatory.

A. TASK: LOSS OF COMMUNICATIONS

REFERENCES: 14 CFR part 91; FAA-H-8083-9, FAA-H-8083-15; FAA-S-8081-4; IAP; AIM.

Objective. To determine that the applicant exhibits instructional knowledge of the elements related to loss of communications by describing:

1. Recognition of loss of communications.
2. When to continue with flight plan as filed or when to deviate.
3. How to determine the time to begin an approach at destination.

B. TASK: APPROACH WITH LOSS OF PRIMARY FLIGHT INSTRUMENT INDICATORS

REFERENCES: 14 CFR part 91; FAA-H-8083-9, FAA-H-8083-15; FAA-S-8081-4; IAP; AIM.

Objective. To determine that the applicant:

1. Exhibits instructional knowledge of the elements related to loss of primary flight instrument indicators by describing—

   a. recognition of inaccurate or inoperative primary instrument indicators and advising ATC and the examiner.
   b. notification of ATC or examiner anytime that the aircraft is unable to comply with an ATC clearance or whether able to continue the flight.
   c. importance of utilizing navigation equipment in an emergency situation and demonstrating a nonprecision approach without the use of primary flight instruments.

2. Exhibits instructional knowledge of common errors related to loss of primary flight instrument indicators by describing—

   a. recognition of failed system components that relate to primary flight instrument indication(s).
   b. failure to notify ATC of situation.
   c. failure to transition to emergency mode/standby instrumentation.

3. Demonstrates and simultaneously explains loss of primary flight instrument indicators by conducting a non-precision approach without the use of these indicators.
4. Analyzes and corrects common errors related to loss of primary flight instrument indicators.

C. TASK: ENGINE FAILURE DURING STRAIGHT-AND-LEVEL FLIGHT AND TURNS

REFERENCES: 14 CFR part 91; FAA-H-8083-9; FAA-S-8081-4; FAA-S-8081-12; FAA-S-8081-14; Aircraft Flight Manual.

Objective. To determine that the applicant:

1. Exhibits instructional knowledge of the elements related to engine failure during straight-and-level flight and turns, solely by reference to instruments, by describing—

    a. appropriate methods to be used for identifying and verifying the inoperative engine.
    b. technique for maintaining positive aircraft control by reference to instruments.
    c. importance of accurately assessing the aircraft's performance capability with regard to action that maintains altitude or minimum sink rate considering existing conditions.

2. Exhibits instructional knowledge of common errors related to engine failure during straight-and-level flight and turns, solely by reference to instruments, by describing—

    a. failure to recognize an inoperative engine.
    b. hazards of improperly identifying and verifying the inoperative engine.
    c. failure to properly adjust engine controls and reduce drag.
    d. failure to establish and maintain the best engine inoperative airspeed.
    e. failure to follow the prescribed checklist.
    f. failure to establish and maintain the recommended flight attitude for best performance.
    g. failure to maintain positive aircraft control while maneuvering.
    h. hazards of exceeding the aircraft's operating limitations.
    i. faulty basic instrument flying technique.

3. Demonstrates and simultaneously explains straight-and-level flight and turns after engine failure, solely by reference to instruments, from an instructional standpoint.
4. Analyzes and corrects simulated common errors related to straight-and-level flight and turns after engine failure, solely by reference to instruments.

D. **TASK: INSTRUMENT APPROACH—ONE ENGINE INOPERATIVE (MULTIENGINE)**

REFERENCES: 14 CFR part 91; FAA-H-8083-9; FAA-S-8081-4; FAA-S-8081-12; FAA-S-8081-14; Aircraft Flight Manual.

Objective. To determine that the applicant:

1. Exhibits instructional knowledge of the elements related to an instrument approach with one engine inoperative by describing—

    a. maintenance of altitude, airspeed and track appropriate to the phase of flight or approach segment.
    b. procedure if unable to comply with an ATC clearance or instruction.
    c. application of necessary adjustments to the published MDA and visibility criteria for the aircraft approach category.
    d. establishment and maintenance of an appropriate rate of descent during the final approach segment.
    e. factors that should be considered in determining whether:

        (1) the approach should be continued straight-in to a landing; or
        (2) a circling approach to a landing should be performed.

2. Exhibits instructional knowledge of common errors related to an instrument approach with one engine inoperative by describing—

    a. failure to have essential knowledge of the information that appears on the selected instrument approach chart.
    b. failure to use proper communications procedures.
    c. noncompliance with ATC clearances.
    d. incorrect use of navigation equipment.
    e. failure to identify and verify the inoperative engine and to follow the emergency checklist.
    f. inappropriate procedure in the adjustment of engine controls and the reduction of drag.
    g. inappropriate procedure in the establishment and maintenance of the best engine inoperative airspeed.
    h. failure to establish and maintain the proper flight attitude for best performance.
    i. failure to maintain positive aircraft control.
    j. faulty basic instrument flying technique.
    k. inappropriate descent below the MDA or DH.
    l. faulty technique during roundout and touchdown.

3. Demonstrates and simultaneously explains an instrument approach with one engine inoperative from an instructional standpoint.
4. Analyzes and corrects simulated common errors related to an instrument approach with one engine inoperative.

X. AREA OF OPERATION: POSTFLIGHT PROCEDURES

A. TASK: CHECKING INSTRUMENTS AND EQUIPMENT

REFERENCES: FAA-S-8081-4; Aircraft Flight Manual.

Objective. To determine that the applicant exhibits instructional knowledge of the elements related to checking instruments and equipment by describing:

1. Importance of noting instruments and navigation equipment for improper operation.
2. Reasons for making a written record of improper operation or failure and/or calibration of instruments prior to next IFR flight.

APPENDIX 1

FLIGHT SIMULATION TRAINING DEVICE (FSTD) CREDIT

TASK VS. FLIGHT SIMULATION TRAINING DEVICE (FSTD) CREDIT

Examiners conducting the instrument rating practical tests with Flight Simulation Training Devices (FSTDs) should consult appropriate documentation to ensure that the device has been approved for training, testing, or checking, and assigned the appropriate qualification level in accordance with the requirements of 14 CFR part 60.

The FAA must approve the device for training, testing, and checking the specific flight TASKS listed in this appendix.

The device must continue to support the level of student or applicant performance required by this practical test standard.

If an FSTD is used for the practical test, the instrument approach procedures conducted in that FSTD are limited to one precision and one nonprecision approach procedure.

USE OF CHART

X   Creditable
A   Creditable if appropriate systems are installed and operating

NOTE: Users of the following chart are cautioned that use of the chart alone is incomplete. The description and objective of each TASK as listed in the body of the practical test standard, including all NOTES, must also be incorporated for accurate FSTD use.

"Postflight Procedures" means closing flight plans, checking for discrepancies and malfunctions, and noting them on a log or maintenance form.

FLIGHT TASK											
Areas of Operation	1	2	3	4	5	6	7	A	B	C	D
Preflight Procedures											
C. Instrument Cockpit Check *				A	A	X	X	X	X	X	X
Air Traffic Control Clearances and Procedures											
A. Air Traffic Control Clearances *				A	A	X	X	X	X	X	X
B. Departure, En Route and Arrival Clearances *				—	—	X	X	X	X	X	X
C. Holding Procedures				—	—	X	X	X	X	X	X
Flight by Reference to Instruments											
A. Basic Instrument Flight Maneuvers				—	—	X	X	X	X	X	X
B. Recovery from Unusual Flight Attitudes				—	—	—	X	X	X	X	X
Navigation Systems											
A. Intercepting and Tracking Navigational Systems and DME ARCS				—	A	X	X	X	X	X	X
Instrument Approach Procedures											
A. Nonprecision Approach (NPA)				—	—	X	X	X	X	X	X
B. Precision Approach (PA)				—	—	X	X	X	X	X	X
C. Missed Approach				—	—	X	X	X	X	X	X
D. Circling Approach				—	—	—	—	X	X	X	X
E. Landing from a Straight-in or Circling Approach				—	—	—	—	—	X	X	X
Emergency Operations											
A. Loss of Communications				—	—	X	X	X	X	X	X
B. One Engine Inoperative during Straight-and-Level Flight and Turns (Multiengine Airplane)				—	—	X	X	X	X	X	X
C. One Engine Inoperative—Instrument Approach (Multiengine Airplane)				—	—	—	—	X	X	X	X
D. Loss of Gyro Attitude and/or Heading Indicators				—	—	X	X	X	X	X	X
Postflight Procedures											
A. Checking Instruments and Equipment				—	A	X	X	X	X	X	X

* Aircraft required for those items that cannot be checked using a flight training device or flight simulator

APPENDIX 2

NON-FSTD DEVICE CREDIT

Deleted.

APPENDIX 3

JUDGMENT ASSESSMENT MATRIX

JUDGMENT ASSESSMENT MATRIX — FLIGHT INSTRUCTOR INSTRUMENT for Airplane and Helicopter		
Acceptable Course of Action — Action of the Applicant Is Acceptable Given the Dynamics of the Flight Environment	Judgment Based Upon the Following SRM Areas	Aeronautical Decision-Making
		Risk Management
		Task Management
		Automation Management
		Controlled Flight Into Terrain
		Situational Awareness
Unacceptable Course of Action — Action of the Applicant Is Unacceptable Given the Dynamics of the Flight Environment	Judgment Based Upon the Following SRM Areas	Aeronautical Decision-Making
		Risk Management
		Task Management
		Automation Management
		Controlled Flight Into Terrain
		Situational Awareness

Areas of Operation:
- I. Fundamentals of Instructing
- II. Technical Subject Areas
- III. Preflight Preparation
- IV. Preflight Lesson on a Maneuver
- V. Air Traffic Control Clearances
- VI. Flight by Reference to Instruments
- VII. Navigation Systems
- VIII. Instrument Approach Procedures
- IX. Emergency Operations
- X. Postflight Procedures

Purpose of the Assessment
To measure the applicant's resource management and judgment skills during the Instrument Pilot practical test

Directions for Completion of the Assessment
1) For each Area of Operation in the Instrument PTS, the applicant can take either an unacceptable or acceptable course of action for the task being evaluated. The examiner should judge use of resource management for each of the resource management areas.

2) For each Area of Operation, mark the column for the course of action that best describes the applicant's decision during that phase of the evaluation. In order to pass, all decisions made by the applicant must be acceptable.

Definitions of Resource Management Areas
Aeronautical Decision Making (ADM)—a systematic approach to the mental process of evaluating a given set of circumstances and determining the best course of action.

Risk Management (RM)—an aeronautical decision-making process designed to systematically identify hazards, assess the degree of risk, and determine the best course of action.

Task Management (TM)—the process pilots use to manage the many concurrent tasks involved in safely operating an aircraft.

Automation Management (AM)—the demonstrated ability to control and navigate an aircraft by correctly managing its automated systems. It includes understanding whether and when to use automated systems, including, but not limited, to the GPS or the autopilot.

Controlled Flight Into Terrain Awareness (CFIT)—the demonstrated awareness of relation to obstacles and terrain.

Situational Awareness (SA)—the use of the resource management elements listed above to develop and maintain an accurate perception and understanding of all factors and conditions related to pilot, aircraft, environment, and external pressures that affect safety before, during, and after the flight.

Reference: FAA-H-8083-9A (Appendix E-1)

Lightning Source UK Ltd.
Milton Keynes UK
UKHW030639310522
403751UK00001B/42